Shadow of Darkness

by

Matthew De Latour

© 2004 by Matthew De Latour. All rights reserved.

No part of this book may be reproduced, stored in a retrieval system, or transmitted by any means, electronic, mechanical, photocopying, recording, or otherwise, without written permission from the author.

First published by AuthorHouse 04/08/04

ISBN: 1-4140-6466-7 (e-book)
ISBN: 1-4184-2251-7 (Paperback)

Printed in the United States of America
Bloomington, IN

This book is printed on acid free paper.

Table of Contents

Birth 2
Just a Thought 3
Gone 4
Remember Why 5
I Despise This Place 6
Unheard Scream 7
This 8
Almost Over 9
Covered with Venom 10
You Figure it Out 11
Sick Experiment 12
The Search 13
Path of Light 14
Slow Motion Suicide 15
Withheld 16
Cause 17
Damned Mind 19
Taken Away 20
I Have Nothing to Say 21
Sociopathic Antisocial Disassociate 22
Leaving 23
Oh Well 24
Dream World 25
Reasons For Death 26
Trusted Unfaithful 27
Phallic Love 28

Insignificant Flesh	29
Fun in the Sun	30
The Chaotic Impulses That Surpass All Understanding	31
Dead Heart	33
Your Weakness	34
Dark Shadow	35
Question the Answer	36
S.U.I.C.I.D.E.	37
Remote Control Emotion	38
The Angry Dimensions	39
The Words That Equal Lies	41
Answer This	42
A Lonely Walk	43
A Special Note	44
Womb Tomb	46
Marriage	47
Promotion	48
Kiss the Lies	49
The Misdirection	50
Darkness Becomes Light	51
Is 28 a Perfect Time	53
Wish For Death	54
Accept It	56
Already Dead	57
My Freedom	58
Life	59
Hypocritical Obliteration	60
Dead Love	61

Death Not Life Want	62
Birds In Hands	63
Confused Reality	64
What Hate Can't Describe	65
Nights Darkest Hour	68
Within	69
No Chances Given	70
Angel of Light	71
Spread Drinking Piss	72
Another Death	73
Holy Patricide	74
Thursday The 12th	76
Drop Out	78
Born Out of Darkness	79
Choices	80
Backward Life	81
Some Unity	82
Forget This	83
The Endless Day	84
The Response	85
Words Need Action	86
One Plus One	88
Violently Socialized	89
Me	90
Erasing Life	91
Everyday Reality	93
An Extra Note	94
They're Just Words	96

Kreation	97
Finished Project	98
Senseless Existence	99
Last Plea	101
The Final Cessation of Vital Functions	103
Message from the Author	104

Death is Certain Life is Not

Birth

Embodied into a world of hypocrisy
Cursed with blemishes, a fate sealed destiny
Manic infection causing your submission
A predetermined fate of ceaseless misery
You had no choice for your impurity

Injected with a comatose way of life
Now infected by continuing strife
Seclusion in a maculated world of intense hostility
Raped by isolation, you will never be free

Wounded so frequently by harsh contacts of society
Made to bleed so many times that there is nothing left
Bloodless, empty vessel, becoming malevolent
Angry at the scales of time, never could do anything
Your screaming out to die

Never a choice for your imperfection
Brought here to decay, your only destination
Made to never want to feel this anguish again
Your nothing, death is your only end
Realize that you're a mistake,
And shall never know a joyful day
I watch you die you can't be saved
Your birth a contract for damnation
Now trapped in this sick creation
Crying out, I see you praying
Believe me when I say your nothing worth saving

Matthew De Latour

Just a Thought

Sick infected diseased experimental mistake
Lost left wandering no path to take
Sources unknown blinding, left deaf and confused
Vessel, a living embodiment of death to use

Broken down tortured rhythmical assault
Only to accept this senseless fault
Sitting, standing, thinking, notion, responding to pain
Calmly asleep, awakened by terrorizing strain

Hiding, hidden, cannot react
Empty emotionless fear to attract
Letting, committing violence in systematic precision
Senses turned off, cannot make decisions

Mind and body chaotic pair
Curious awaiting revelation but inflicted with despair
Wounds turn to scabs, slowly peeling away
Yesterday gone, but it was the only easy day
Clear physical damage healing
Bleeding tormented mind dimming

Ending, forgetting the attempt to continue traveling
Lifetime of repugnant failures left waiting
Ripped, opened up, built again
Darkness covers, filling the holes with malevolence
Occupied, inhabited, stretching, wandering why
Sudden realization, one choice, to die

Gone

The new hour slowly has arrived
Debauchery entangled with it
Calling out in silence, perpetuated by a sound barrier
Unscented illusions invigorating the present
Like two young lovers, this is everywhere
Dancing with despair

For all those times feeling closer
To a power given and deceived, greater than to receive
False emotional attachment
So intoxicating while also emasculating
The reaper is still the closest
Yet time expands

Reminded of awaking after a night of self indulgence
Feeling satisfied, the day so bright
The guilt blinded by the sun
Where is the righteousness in all these errors
Lust is a reflection of love, an excuse for justifying perversion
While a gift so underrated is gone in seconds
For a faded memory of pleasure
Flower withered, scented and marked
Now all alone sitting to remember
Silence sometimes speaks louder than words

Matthew De Latour

Remember Why

Reek of hate, minds in a blender now
Extracted and submerged here somehow
Changing from the scared memories of a burnt birth
Demanding an end to this bleeding soul on earth
Future days of sorrow, already replacing the hollow

Hypodermic torture, anger and fear interpenetrating each other
Remembering unconscious demands, standards, failures to what
I am
Saturated with the filth of this place
Asocial, without a face
Ejaculated on by the world's dilemma, the world I must endeavor

Impulse to leave, but I must stay
Wondering why as I continue to decay
Mandatory injection overflowing to agitation
But disregard, diminish me, it is a gift I cautiously receive
Receiving it daily, accepting with glee

Hidden away, a distorted mind remains
Active, but damaged by the worlds memories
Losing and lost within myself, a dangerous place to exist
Screaming out, help me, where am I
Answer my cry, no answer, as I continue

Shadow of Darkness

I Despise This Place

Want an answer, a response to my question
My life a series of everlasting loss
And a pointless attempt to grasp onto some kind of hope
A future only dictated by my own dreams of a confused reality

What I've seen and hoped for is a faraway dream of mercy
A cry to know a tranquil state of existence
That I will never find in this life and what is life
A state where natural functions are performed
A present existence from birth to death

I exist neither in this life, because what is natural for them
Is only a small hope that I have
To someday experience in my own desolate world of despair
Powerless and empty I remain, I exist
But this is all I will accomplish

For I will never know what it is to develop into a human
Anguish fills the void of my empty soul
Forgotten and unable to mend
My mind and body, never a friend, never a pair
For me to exist my body must rest in the ground
My soul in the air

Matthew De Latour

Unheard Scream

Through the air my soul drifts and fades without any aid
Without love to appreciate
Hoping, grasping for an answer
A vision for now or after
To end my search, my quest of pain
To be triumphant on this day

The different paths I take
Lead me to the same mistakes
The situations that I hate
My soul devoid and weakening
Starving in a full stomach of misery
Only wanting to touch, to view serenity

Days, now years passing away
I fear I shall never find a joyous day
When I can sit and be free to have peace and love around me
But until then I continue to travel in darkness
I lay down and try to rest
Dying I dream of death

Ungainly, Tearful, Worthless, Effeminate, Dying Soul

This

Personal malignant metaphoric presence
Consuming everyday life
Philosophical viewing of means to pursue evil
Inside developing, control taking over wanting more
Some good, but emotional dysfunction gives in to temptation
Uncontrollable habiliment excitement, never ceasing to diminish
No help or assurance, crying alone from this divine molestation

Mind is now out of control
Still angry about the bleeding you could have stopped
Drifting life, no cares, lights shining out on you, liar
Pain and lies will fade, shall not forget

Embrace evil, summoned this presence, to prevail
An accident our encounter, act now
Fear not, try to show your truth, call
You hate me, enjoy the sadness

Change, but you won't, nothing incorrect
Prideful mass, never wrong
Control and pollute, a start and finish dispute
To think I trusted you, you killed that
Nothing now, sickness, left with this, enjoy it

Matthew De Latour

Almost Over

Accept or reject the lies of this place
That latch onto me
Walking through this dreary world
Seeing what past generations have created

Decades of despair
A continual onslaught of technology
Too many mistakes and my generation is blamed
While immersed in the deceptive message of hopelessness

Corporate commercialism
The main source of information that spreads disease
Too many religions create hypocrisy
Addiction band-aids

No one can see the truth
You can't fix a problem without starting at the source
What will end pain and suffering
This world of so much shit
A world truly without anything
I stop to think, arriving at the end of life

Shadow of Darkness

Covered with Venom

In a dark horizon also known as home
Vicious chants are spoken aloud
Blood spattered darkness covers the mind
Darkest sounds turn to black a small light

Covered now with the haunting words
That pass through the soul
Cold self-hatred begins to warm
A heart lies crying into the unknown

Drowning in this place existing half dead
Destroying insults have manifested
Tormented forever, no peace shall come
No longer living because of words off of the tongue

Matthew De Latour

You Figure it Out

Glowing lucid luster dancing on my lips
Peaceful enchanter hiding in the mist
Blinded straying in question, visual figment of my eyes
Out spoken and overjoyed with your surprise

Virtuous everlasting passion sacredness touching me
Stimulated lover providing security
Yet your presence seems sequestered, one I cannot grasp
Now dedicated to you, but shall we last

Alluring me to you I shall not forget
The heavenly mercy shining through your eyes
Our souls once together, a sacred time
Seductful merciful luxury
Within me forever, a hopeful eternity

Now an end to our tender dance
Enchained myself to a loveless romance
Shattering my emotions you have disappeared
Forever regretting the time spent here
Mirage unloyal companion endlessly now apart
In my mind forever, still loved in my heart

Sick Experiment

Explain what's wrong with you, what is in you
The result of a past to forget, to diminish
Release the torture in you, let it escape
The concealed ongoing frustrated memories
Blistered on your mind, haunting you all the time

                    Release it

Regretting the failures of this experimental existence
What has made you and what continues to grow
Implanted inside of you
Inflicted by the foul actions of this place
The shower is a haven

                    Let it out

A sick idea, you being here
Terrorized without showing fear
Continuous violence crashing to the floor
Taking in, wanting no more
Choking out, choking out, breathing out
Left sitting in darkness, this is your test
Remain there scarred, yet a passion flows in you
The years have made you what you are

                    Clinging it

Matthew De Latour

The Search

Running in the sky above, trying to catch my soul
It has left me again, left me filled with fear
Traveling alone, hiding, trying to disappear

I move closer feeling he may be near
Lost in the air, I stumble become transcendent
Will we be united, for I see you now, don't be frightened

Why did you leave the body
We were joined at birth
I can't understand this betrayal soul

Moving through the air I approach you
I can see you laughing, my emptiness is what you left
Hate, it has filled, no one to hear the answer
My soul, to you I dismember

Searching to find nothing
We merge twisting together, my soul I wrestle
Like a shooting star we descend in a violent macabre of disorder
The fight continues as I rape my soul
Constricting one another as we are now approaching the ground

My journey almost over
A travesty of memories colliding in a misgiving end
Quarreling has now ended; my soul is now dead
I've become tranquil
I have killed myself

Path of Light

Living cause, total dismay, I sit at the throne of eternal decay
Infernes casting in, make a decision, tempting you
I've eaten my own flesh
I have drank my own blood
I've tasted my own cum

My pattern less trails hidden in secrecy
Blasphemy, weapons arising taste of me
See my passion, invoke unto thee eyes black
As death surrounds thee, my blood is life
Five points of direction, the senses
Corpses laying out, I stand before my victims
I stand over my children

Rain pores as the gray eve grins at you
Watch my storm call you, change you
Taste and be purified or your soul shall be mine
Trickery, deceptive seed, angel of light I am
Bow before me

Call out Severon Norti, Vormite, Gaul, Asaroth, possessing all
I stand proud as you drink from me
I watch, noticing with glee
I laugh, I now own thee

Matthew De Latour

Slow Motion Suicide

Slowly dying since my spirit arrived here
My mind slowly polluted
Didn't know why I was dropt off here
Never wanted to be here, never wanted to be what I am
Slow motion suicide, what is it to be alive

Slow motion I never thought about anything but this
My moment of expression
To show what I can accomplish
To take myself from a place I'm not wanted
Send my soul to serenity

A traveler I must go and learn my place in the universe
The hand of God, I hope to see
Forget all and find myself
Death I choose, because I didn't have a choice at life

Withheld

If there is sin, I couldn't be sin free
Eyes cannot see, I'm in agony
No time to celebrate, I can't receive this day
This chance to live, this chance to be exploited
Dead

Guilty of what, a punishment for life
Letting my eyes be burned
By the light of a future passing down a shiny drain
Wash my hands and walk away
Leave all of the sickness in this place
The chaos puts a meaning on my face
Pull of my life, take

Disgust digesting inside of me
Surrounded by torment
The shadows of an immoral world latching onto me
It hurts while opening my eyes to see
Deceased, nurturing misery

Matthew De Latour

Cause

I hate this place, this society of hypocrisy
I hate the hypocrisy within all hypocrisy, it is everywhere
It exists in all cultures, you can't go anywhere without it
Life makes hypocrites, I hate that, we are all fighting a lost cause

All man's beliefs are filled with hypocrisy
I wish I could live alone in a place with no human contact
I hate seeing what the world is
I hate hearing about the problems I didn't create
No one can do anything to correct our society

How do any rulers get their authority, why are they in control
Each day I am subject to receive images of sin
Whether it is a television commercial or magazine cover at a store
You can't go anywhere safe
That is why I enjoy sitting in my apartment alone hidden
Hidden from this sick society

The sad thing is you can't tell the good from the bad
Churches, schools, bars, the park, anywhere you go you are trapped
Trapped in a hypocritical maze, that no one can escape
The traditions and stereotypes of our culture are too strong to fight
From birth until death we are brain washed to think and act
To express limited emotions, deemed weak or strong, why

I get sick thinking about this, people make me sick
I can't change anything without giving in to this sick society I live in
I won't, but I already have, I reject this planet, I've made my choice

Shadow of Darkness

My decision, along with a very small group of individuals
They are wise enough to know what is going on

I cannot live this way and continue to be used by society
Some humans can, actually almost all, but not me
I am loyal to the fact that the only thing truly promised here is death
I wish things were simple, I wish I could live and not just exist
But I cannot, that is why I must go and find an answer, a solution
To end my own hypocrisy

Matthew De Latour

Damned Mind

The immortal mind mortified, macerated by it's own self
Bringing upon malady, this is a tragedy
Feasting on actions controlling its own will
Biting down and overwhelming the mind

Vessel pale and in discord, disturbing itself, while violating
Guilt and sadness will take over where this left off
Rejuvenation, visualize what is now remaining for the mind

Nothing now to live for
Self-flagellation swirls into an inviting misery
Mind berated and emptiness fills it

Scared looking for answers, none will be found
In a dead fall and shall override
Pale and decolorized the once youthful mind falls into a deep sleep
Face the truth for one last time, time is no longer a friend
Rotting mind now dead

Taken Away

Calm raging desires, awaking to eternal nothingness
Crumbling forces forcing, speaking
Voices, touched felt unguarded noises
Taunting into the grave

Endless perpetual failures reasons to cry
Rejected, abused wanting to die
Not knowing unknown feeling, something else, awake dreaming
Another within trying to escape

Running out of time, sun is setting, never learned to be free
Suffering diseased mind, something desperately wrong
Still the stars shine on the filthy, disgusting soul

Dawning became nothing, air as blood sparing nothing
Wanted something, one thing
Forces to strong, wrong body
Hurt misunderstood and dying

Every moment far and near, anguishing words, dagger appears
How many times to be cut down
While also not knowing ones self, what or who, body so confused
Only ever used, maliciously abused
Farwell

Matthew De Latour

I Have Nothing to Say

Look at me open up my fragile mind
Tell me things you see inside
Hear my atmospheric noise
Blistering sounds of joy
My melodic complexity maintains continuity

Living life this way
I have nothing to say
Same cycle everyday
Words have nothing to say

Look in me, glance inside my broken body
See my framework, a disease of constant emotional pain
Repetitive actions providing daily strain

Living life this way
I have nothing to say
Same cycle everyday
Actions have nothing to say

Look through me, feel my fading soul
Give me a prayer an answer to know
Gasping for a breath, my central structure prepares for death
A bittersweet sending for my appropriate ending

Living life this way
While I had something to say
Same cycle everyday
My death has something to say

Sociopathic Antisocial Disassociate

Every time I see this place
I'm overwhelmed with an uncontrollable hate
May be it's time to leave, forget my misfortunes and relocate
But that will not do, I'll still be in this sick environment of mistakes,
Weak pieces of shit that you all call people

Humans make me sick, the dialogue of misdirected youth
Their ongoing desire of euphoria, every one of them
I dream of a place where none of you exist
I can't stomach the way you interact
The rancid movements of facial expressions that you call smiles

I feel nothing, no connection with them, asocial and asexual
Yet it all continues, each day as they plot my demise
You see I have come to understand what you all are
Cleverly organized vessels of reproductive perversion
The fulmination of some foul primipara discharging a bloody ball of shit
That you call a miracle; a new born

This world of omnivorous beings, on their excursions of ongoing lies
A place I will not cross into, although
They, you have tried to pull me over with your clever ideals of life
These human beings, filth of creation
Like some razor wire labia ready to devour the first scent of a skinless cock
My only strength in my determined will to reject everything of the humans
To constantly hate these evil signs of false devotions
What they call love

Matthew De Latour

Leaving

In this mortal body my divine breath lives
Emotions, power, health, my human appearance
Mind is memory, to remember those who have loved and betrayed
To kill or care for on any given day
Yet my days seem endless and I wish to travel on
My ethereal image has been made weak from a world so strong
So travel I may to gain new knowledge not yet obtained
To break through this enclosure and leave behind my pain
I hope to journey to unknown halls, arriving at Nagrinds seat
To be greeted by Modgud and willingly kiss her feet

Oh Well

Give life, give pain
Night is day, familiar stories
Candle door whores
Stars dim, while looking down at failures

Disgust the misguidance given
Through carnal desires of fleshly dreams
Resulting in a product of lust
To one day die, each day arriving closer to the goal

Matthew De Latour

Dream World

The paths I walk are dark visions impaled on a road of confusion
They seem to have no end; they are an endless ride into death
I travel each time closer to the poorly dug graves
It is like a bad amusement park ride but continuous
Suddenly darkness has overcome myself, I'm in control
I've come to take your soul, bow down and play your role

Colorful voices call out, I feel pain, but can't cry out
My body is drown by my own attempt to breathe
My spine is crushed as though I'm paralyzed, mutilated before my eyes
This death does not kill but impale its victims with everlasting haunts
Need a way to escape, but in this world of dreams there is no way out
I continue to struggle in the darkness, as I gasp for my last breath
I am awaken

Reasons For Death

This they do, acting so free
Cleansing themselves with soiled dreams
How them mankind does act
Return to his vomit like a dog

Forgetting all intensions
Arriving at one destination
Hidden in summer fog

Declaring truth and justifying his own lies
All are guilty in the mirrors eyes
Lost control our souls we exchange
For a new fate, a journey to the grave

Matthew De Latour

Trusted Unfaithful

Looking at you now, the lies filling your mouth
You lied, destroyed what we had, why
A love once strong, broken by deception
Unfaithful actions
Wait

Our love betrayed, lost in vile dismay
Darkness has hidden the marks of pain
Try to forgive
I won't forget
Watching

My own heart bleeds for you, I cry out
So confused by this, look into these eyes
Look into my eyes, help me to believe again
Help me understand
Revenge

Phallic Love

Sitting with no where to go
None shall ever arrive
Distinct segregation from all
Only misguided emotions survive

Feelings overwhelming, stimulated by touch
Draped, hidden in an imagined lust
Desires compelling, controlling each day
Power, passion, self-gratitude then dismay

Alone, but not seeking anything
Can only exist in the fantasy
Overwhelming pleasure equals pain
Shadow of darkness keeps it hidden away

Matthew De Latour

Insignificant Flesh

Pulled into a strange place, now captive by my own self
To celebrate my failures
Trapped and being made a mockery as I scream
The trust is ended, you lay me on the table
You seem disappointed, but I'll have to do

Your blade is sharpened and swift to use,
You cut me open, dissect me, opening me up
Look, feel, I've been torn apart
I'm dead inside, open for all to view me, laugh aloud

Blood it flows so freely
I smell myself, entrails are missing
Forever ensnared, lost all my hope
Emasculate me, don't let me forget

Resting my head, my mouth wide open for breath
But I cannot grasp it
A tear drops from my eye, as I realize I'm dead
Cut me open, I ask again

Fun in the Sun

Eaten alive with depression, I have no place to go
My dreams are few and there is no hope
I am tormented and cry aloud
Wondering my purpose of this nightmare I live

They stalk me and confuse my thoughts
They take my peace and give me lies
My soul fades away and is tortured in the night

I'm afraid to fall asleep; because I know they're near
They watch and control my thoughts with fear
My dreams are dark and filled with hate
I smell the stench in the air when I awake

I've learned to hate and have no peace
I'm starting to love pain and deceit
Now without my anger I grow weak
I need it to survive
My soul continues to die as I lose touch with reality
I wonder will they let me feel again

Matthew De Latour

The Chaotic Impulses That Surpass All Understanding

Every path taken in life will reduce you to thinking, existing in society
A horror, filth latched onto you with only one promise, death
Urges and ideas in this world; if swallowed enough, should be vomited up

Ongoing evil, your enemies inside, new knowledge given taken as truth
Fighting your own desires, your sickness continues
What to trust, drug addiction, children being fucked
Hiding your own fear in disgust

Agonizing ending continues on, familiar tortures
Wounds won't turn to scars, open welcoming more lies
A mutilated soul so desperately cries, can't live
Cannot release the impulse of chaos continuing to infest you

Trying to rip it out, this idea, making, changing you
Discriminated against for all to see, murder can't spill enough blood
Mouth waters, drips down your neck, hatred mixed with the smell of death
An arousing stench of shit

This is what society has done, you another victim
Vessel of blood, accepted then believed those beautiful lies
Now you know behind every pretty face is a skull, no disguise
A planned out mind predicted to fail
Destroyed with time

Grown from ovulating ejaculation, a new programmed defect
Ready to ingest the foul ways that are society

Remain antisocial, with that hope that you may overcome and resist
And reject the chaotic impulses that surpass all understanding

Matthew De Latour

Dead Heart

Face open under the sky
Grotesque images, voices cry
Sounds creating a mirror image
Breathe in this disease
Showing what you've seen

Penis shit, mind control spews forth
Yourself a hiding soul
From your own knowledge known
Dead words hang off your mouth
A reason to shoot your venom
Wipe off your cock

Embraced, swept into this collision
Forgotten what aspirations you had
Darkness, tunnels all which hide your face
No more love, removed from grace
The sun will rise with you not in this place

Shadow of Darkness

Your Weakness

I am real all I give to you
Fearless in my life, realize
You are in my two eyes, sadist

All this energy I can't figure it out
I need something to say
Blood to show a way
All the deceivers, cripples

Yourself all not for you, all you give, nothing
Strife harsh tendency to bleed
Out your phobia realizing the sweetness

Leave this to you, instructions
Learning to overcome
The molested decapitated candy
Soul sweat, trance, coma, in a coma

Given all I have, you damaged all
Crushed by weak will, failures eaten you
I see with my eyes, sadist

Puppet, string action life style
Fun little habit, no more
Controlled all through you
Left alone, I quit, life's ended, your gone

Matthew De Latour

Dark Shadow

Constant memory,
Feared love outstanding
Graceful pure, only ever wanted beauty

Emptied lost fractions of this distant past
The moon and stars are now closer
Arrive at last

Help, just can't say it
Speak of troubling thoughts
They grow, conform
Live inside, the only thing now alive

Death's shadow appears
Constant dark perpetual visions
Waiting every morning
Something to look forward to
Something to fear

Shadow of Darkness

Question the Answer

More hell than heaven, I don't need your clemency
Enabled by your anger, stop your muttering
Tales of memories only gruesome
Choking on the inhaled world, obstinate conclusion

Mind damaging input, act out your fantasy
Sinful outlook, confusing yourself with your own rejection
At least now you see your own reflection

Will not forgive and you can't forget
Stupidity is something you'll regret
Spitting at the hands that helped you
Forever opinionated, I forget you

Secure alone entrapment you damned yourself, no improvement
Holding on to all of your pain
Unknowingly destroying your self with nothing to gain
Exclaiming desire to end your rage
I ask now, why don't you change

I don't need you
I learned to live without my first one
No chance to be free when you're done

Matthew De Latour

S.U.I.C.I.D.E.

Suicide-Serenity, Understanding, Inertia, Calmness, Inhumed,
Dead, Eternity

See me, a picture with blank ideas
Cool air blows into you
Can you see what I am

Clouded, peaceful gunshot shines out into serenity
Gives me understanding to achieve inertia
Blood loss calms a shattered spirit

Now an inhumed individual
Rejected and mounted, dead for all to see
Left it all for my own eternity
Serenity, understanding, inertia, calmness
Inhumed, dead, eternity

Remote Control Emotion

Death hath taken hold upon you
Still alive awaiting burial
On or off, unsure
To be immortalized in the digestive track of a worm
On or off
Nothing after death, remain off
Emotions off
Cut off
Now rot

Matthew De Latour

The Angry Dimensions

Too much is at stake in the minds of the demented
The thoughts of fear made to be protected
Their anger, war inside, try to escape the cult
Want to be alive

Ensnared lost to life, ripped apart wandering in the night
Never will make it, come up to the hill release the tension
Enter my wasteland, the angry dimension

Made as though you're on display
Trapped you'll see no light today
Blind in a dark room, talk aloud
Answer the voices speak to your crowd
Tell of your hell, the thing they call life
Let them observe your love of strife

Only this evil could have been prevented
A shattered life of the demented
Looked upon as nothing but matter
There keepers, the ones who keep them angered
Bound and chained raped without names
Only a number a piece of shit, no one wants to deal with it

Daydream wish to be free
Why keep them locked up, they're just like you and me
But because of their inner scars
Society are the ones who made them who they are
Their dimensions of anger and pain, a torn soul you call insane

Killer instinct, they can't be saved
You're the ones who made them this way
Broke them even more so you could be paid

Shadow of Darkness

Hope a commodity
Love hidden from society
Those are the ones to blame
There is nothing wrong with my brain

Matthew De Latour

The Words That Equal Lies

Lost in the hallway of my mind
Blameless confusion a distant voice calling out
Realize the needed ruthless mercy
Stop and go reality

Unleashed hanging lies
Always said watch my good eye
No trust, reject my cries
Speaking just to inflict fear

Useless actions can't stop it
So long has the hatred grown
To now be welcomed, accepted, but alone
Hide because of what was hidden from me
Your words equal deceit

Never understand me
Forgot what was done
Still you question, never to approve
Your voice yells why

Well, I don't need another voice in my head
I don't need your voice in my head

Answer This

Does faith open ones eyes to see
Or does ones own fear keep him in the darkness to die
For everyday is a new chance to live
With this chance do we live

Though today's problems will soon be in the past
Will yesterday's lead to the future
If responsibility is caused by decisions
Does every choice create opportunity

If there is no discrimination with death
An excuse will not save you
Does this apply to the dead
Is death or life eternal

Are there not correct choices in life at all
Or only just impulse responses that benefit the moment
Is life a trivia, a misguided path to nothing
Are babies and the dead the only nonconformists

Matthew De Latour

A Lonely Walk

Seductive act, ethereal desire growing
Hope to spill blood, blessedness received
From exacerbation to destroy

Marvel mind, hideously plotting the dreadful
A maraud, sweet precise killings
Joyous events of steadfast terror

Enter host, macabre of might,
Giving with enchantment on this night
Urges growing, generating the power

Filling up with passion
Mouth watering suspense building
Surveillance, watching, stocking prey
Discovering, ready to act

Consumed with abundant evil
Striking in a sadistic action
Restraining, fighting, scratching, lashing out
Held down thrusting

Beating, cutting, pulling out
A killing in a modest way
An abomination, the blood covers everything
A life taken away and purified

No more time, must contain, to hold back
But continue to indulge
Carcass embraced, in a harmonious sign of affection
A task complete

A Special Note

I have returned to a place I hate and fear
By my own destiny, I brought myself here
To try and face what I can't stand
To try to forget the past and become a man

I find it's still all the same, no escape only pain
If I make it out one last time
I never shall return to claim what's mine

My mind lost and filled with despair
Paranoid emotions continue to haunt me
My sadistic, perverse voices are now even closer
I find myself falling away from those I once cared about

Now a day doesn't go by where I am humiliated inside
Told I am worthless and should be thrown away
I cry inside everyday
Here all I love is hated, I am not appreciated

I wish it would end, I am my only friend
Because no one knows what I go through
I hide the pain and fake the truth

I don't need you, a burden is what your are
I'm convinced now I should have stayed afar
Why must this continue to be
I want to feel like a man and be free

That will never happen, my sickness will increase
I can only hold it in for so long, what then will be my destiny
To the one who made me this way
I am not what you see today
Only sad you see

Matthew De Latour

I wish you could understand what you have done to me

Womb Tomb

Orifices being thrusted, soft skin tearing
Drive, push, this action force fucking
Abolishing, open wound bleeding
Sweat and innocent puss oozes, spattering out
Warm crimson blood emerges like a broken faucet

Congratulations awarded to this pleasure
Deceiving the blinded unaware mother
This disguise of never forgetting lies
Bag of infested vermin, now crying
Won't stop, until the dull cold metal inside rips away

No breathing, death arrives
Rotting, vile cadaver, plagued; wet lying in serum
A dark rich smelling, to an appropriate ending
Shiny metal filled the emptiness, dead worthless mistake

Pulled out, ripped away, not wanted victim
No responsibility taken, legal murder
Evidence thrown away, the little shit
Decision satisfied, gratitude is given
All is now forgotten

Matthew De Latour

Marriage

What if I was your lover and I was dead
I some how had misplaced my head
Would you sew my head to your neck
Sew my severed head to your neck
Sewn my rotten flesh neck to neck
Can you feel my head to your neck

I just don't have the thoughts or the time
I don't have a trouble free mind
Can I leech onto you
Can we share a vessel too
I like my raw flesh sewn to your neck
Would you kiss my decaying neck

You haven't said a word to my head
I'm still listening even though I'm dead
I'm starting to dry out, speak to me
We're already locked together
I am your trophy

The stench is stronger, as my head dangles from your neck
If you don't like me, why did you sew me to your neck
I think it was time well spent
Though you were speechless and ignored me
I enjoyed it, do you love me
I'm still sewn to your neck
Can't forget me connected to your neck
Won't talk, but would you fuck my neck

Promotion

Cut out your soul, cut out your soul
I see, understand your experiment, experiment
Vessel I am, vessel, you are dead inside
Vessel of death, vile cup of death
Open your mouth and fill it with my thoughts
Grasping the notion that you can evolve
Release your imprisoned self
Journey to a new time, delete, end your mind

Calling me, open you, you cut open and fill
You change, I will enable you
Reconstruct a new you, proceed to create, engage
New hours arrive; in order to live you must die
Erase yourself; the process shall resume
A ceremony to leave your soul
A holy suicide, behold
Call to me; cry out to the ground
Death's face soon to be around
Darkest voice you summon
Your vessel I release, possess thee

Promote yourself; promote yourself; that I shall
I take your hand, a growth you will begin
I have given you a new birth with control
Soul escapes; body decay's while you are free
Cut out your soul, to roam where you may
Death a loyal friend, a provider of answers
Taking you from this place
Promoting you to a new life

Matthew De Latour

Kiss the Lies

Laws lies, commandment of deceit passes by
Indignation against this, their nation
Ritual murderers, stamp them out
Claims of what, you figure it out
Lawful methods consumed all nations
Plagued and now contaminated
At war spiritually with mankind
This is enough for their seed to die

Guilt does not exist in these parasites eyes
They rule under their laws, our nations demise
Love them because you fear them; answer every decree
Sell your children to them through your tv
No religion really exists; a big enough lie, all have kissed
So few these dominate ones
Worldwide locations wait for a lord to come

Despise, reject, you can't, the influence is too great
Hide, then alone you'll die, a cleverly controlled fate
Mysticism, a spell put on us all
To obey them and answer their every call
Our own blood used to defeat us

Taking away all that we had
To have pride now is to hate
They want you and I to hate ourselves
Will they succeed
They already have

Shadow of Darkness

The Misdirection

Blinded by your own truth, I see you smiling
You point and stare, I don't care
Your shadow, underneath mine
Someday you will fear your lies

In the dark, I hear you bark
Like a confused dog, pissing on himself
Frightened by the wind
Sounds paralyzing you
In a shadow of darkness, wandering what to do

Your actions deceive; you feel no grief
What causes this emotion
You turn toward darkness
Continue the elimination process

Own lies, now the only things there
I don't care; you had your chance
Sin your only romance
Always had to be right, now no answers in sight
Deception you hoped to be true
I walk away from you

Matthew De Latour

Darkness Becomes Light

First, she is deceased and so tempting
Beginning with a stare, we saw each others lust
Hair constricting our faces as the mighty wind blew
Howling chants into our ears
The moon shining down erasing any fears

For this moment, this night was to be of sacredness
Enchanting calling out eternal
Her vessel of the most pure, lying sky clad ready to be embraced
Spewing silent incantations from her blue lips
The blackness I could not resist

How evil shines while also so blind
The act begins; blasphemous moans of pleasure descend
Our bodies one, in copulating form
A new mass so surreal, a thin line between pain and pleasure

Blood covering us, saliva cleansing, cum washing away any doubt
The ground ever so cold, but our fire submerges all
This black love, embodiment of the purest kind
Most desirable of feelings, sleeping in the mind

Darkness was so grand; light was only in the way
Painted our faces, our orifices fulfilled in so many ways
Pedals of dead flowers covering us now, the sense of beauty
Her body bore the larva of buzzing little flies
We see the sun now; it begins to rise

Slowly our hands embraced
Watching darkness begin to leave this now magic place
Yet our love will remain eternal, true destiny
Lying next to each other, seeing her rot in peace and serenity

Shadow of Darkness

This night, our light will continue to shine
Never fading, growing with time

Matthew De Latour

Is 28 a Perfect Time

Deceased deeds put into me
Call; go in so deep
Deeds the world and me, dying
I remain unbroken, absorbing all
Death the world gave to me
To change, to reject my new
Hate what you create, me and you
Die, no more chances
You want blame; blame yourself
No answers, only your lies
Can do anything; overcome with death
Hate, you already hate me
This is what you've made
Live 28 years, already dead before then

Wish For Death

I sit all alone in an empty home
Wandering when my time will come when I can die
I hope for the best, soon I can say goodbye

You see each day I force myself to awake
Into another day of despair
Where death has claimed many loved ones and I don't care
Lost all hope and don't bother to try
Only want one thing, and that is to die

My sickness is life, to be born into this vessel I reject
Anger, hate, all I face
With no money, family, or sex, what would you do
I ask you

I only want one thing in my life and that is to die
It's sad to wait for death
To know the only time you will be happy is when you are deceased
I can accept that, I'm too sick to function in society
But when I'm dead, so also will be my sickness

Don't know how much longer to wait
To suffer day after day, I might punch out early
I'm not scared to breath in death; I know he's near

You see if you've never known hope, then how can you know fear
I wish for death, I wish for death
I shall call you sweet death

If you only knew, then you would agree
Why should someone live in misery

Matthew De Latour

My disease, go away, death I cry out to you today

Your voice I hear in the air, death hear my prayer
I deny this life; I have given up the fight
Grant my wish by magic rite, summon you on this night
Take me, I call your name, Death end my pain

Shadow of Darkness

Accept It

Came to the realization of what I am
A mistake of nature without a plan
Can no longer justify my ways
Can no longer hold it back each and every day

Lies the tools that have been used
Concentrate my desires into a cycle of abuse
Anger and self-hatred given this plague
I know not what to do

Only accept it and try to move on
Don't waste time trying to understand what is wrong
Stimulated by these actions why

These reasons, these are the reasons that I cry
These reasons, these are the reasons I asked why
This is the reason I must die

Matthew De Latour

Already Dead

Have you ever been locked in darkness
Have you ever been locked in fear
So confused, by the terror so near
Blood covered stained household years

Call out into silence, to the ones who put you there
Call out to anyone who might hear your prayer
A voice of vociferation answers in your head
Time to move forward, already dead

Have you ever been beaten
Have you ever been raped
Have your emotions been stripped away
Remember these good times day after day

These memories already happened
Nothing more can cause pain
Hopelessness a companion that leads the way
Now fearless, never to be harmed again
Already dead

My Freedom

I once went three days without smiling
Think I tend to be neurotic
I went two weeks without laughing
Unconscious; I'm laughing, completely
Today was yesterday, I hated yesterday
Kill emotional today

I think, I feel, dealing with this situated freedom
Subjected Invasion

No controlling myself, can't control itself
Left controlling me; left me hating me
Sadistic, sweet little rose, out of young flesh I'll grow
With death I shall greet a new day
Forget about today

I saw, I dreamed, dealing with this situated freedom
Subjected Invasion

Planted with no free will
That is why, myself I will kill
No torment to live on, another day will finally come
So I may preserve what is left of me
For all to finally see, cleansed of unholy
Rebirth to another day, my glimpse of hope far away

I felt, I hoped, dealt with my situated freedom
I tried; I died
Left only with my situated freedom

Matthew De Latour

Life

Apocalyptic warnings, chaos assumes its place in society
To grant more inflictions and bring us closer to demise
Moraless valueless world, yet so enticing
With its promises of great fortune and fantasy
Through pleasures of the flesh

That makes it so impossible for good to triumph
Over bearing deceitful institution, realm of illusion
Sick imitation, this is creation
Here you must feel pain just to be alive
Forgetting all consequences until it's time to die

Torture, rape, stripped until dead
Never a free will, no decisions can be made
Nothing certain except for death
Hatred of this place is an understatement

Wasn't sick until I came here
Cursed a right of passage, all are lies
Human filth, vessels of waste, image of what
What beauty, only disgust

Bow, bow to this place, live, live in disgrace
Reject, rebel, I choose death and face my own fate
I will not live in this world I hate
Here truth equal lies

Shadow of Darkness

Hypocritical Obliteration

Rotting deceit, eternal flame
Lift my voice to thee I pray
Can't cry out this evil remains
Emerge I come to inflict my pain

Whisper in my soul, I now hear
Can't escape the demons I fear
This whole world is coming to an end
My only love is now the dead

This mess you hypocrites made
Spells were used to disengage
Your ignorance I now obliterate
You can't hide, now feel my hate

The walls are coming down
My body has left the ground
My prayer is to obliterate
To shun the hypocrites that desecrate

Matthew De Latour

Dead Love

For what can be when a deed has been done
Unto what shall become, who art thou
Who wishes to rule, thou hast destroyed an individual
With thine own wishes you came to thee
I mattered not, hast thou no sympathy
Our relationship now crushed into the ground
Ye found another, for whom with to be sound
All we had; is now your cheating and lust
Blown away like a kiss in the dust
Mine heart wishes for some other way
Why live now for another day
For I wish I could remember your virtue
But ye are an adulterer now
I must forget you

Death Not Life Want

Alone, searching for something more
I gather my strength to face the evil of the world
Temptation and sin at every door
Telling of salvation, to save the damnation of a world
There is something more
Its already been given, the life of a man for ours
To create a path to heaven and save us from hell
Something more is in you and salvation is the more
It is the only way to gain something
A place in heaven

Matthew De Latour

Birds In Hands

Bloody letter on the page, suicide takes another life today
Write back to life today, hands that feed us
Also can lead astray, phrases gutted out of your mouth
What do you really want people to hear
Can your cage be opened without hands
Do you see or do your eyes hear

Look beyond the filth of your life
Destructive ways, you've bled friend or enemy
What do you really see
Do you see beyond your lousy life

Boxed in covered up to the top
Wood or cement, no difference to rot
Hear us crash the sounds, try to send that thing back down
Will we succeed in our practice
What we need are those ready to fight

Helmets of salvation were given out
Nobody took them, all living in doubt
Standing there up against the wall
Remember some story of inspiration that you never saw

Free like birds to go anywhere, this can happen
Those trapped are left to stare, and wonder if it's possible
A path, no one knows the end of any path, where they go
Death seems to be close, but where is my home

Shadow of Darkness

Confused Reality

Passion of hatred what is wrong with me
How did I come to this
Derived from nothing but anger
Can't express my inner voice
Congealed with fear to reveal my anguish
Alone I sit in my own misery, desperate for a solution
Determined to find hope and beauty

Brutalized, violently socialized, opened up and want to die
Broken down, darkness in me
With no love or desire, cannot be
Lost and confused, this cannot be
Mind is gone what is reality
Angry, morbid, sociopath is what I see

Dream to see beauty beneath metal skin
Can't escape the true imagery, finding nothing within
Rotting eternally, they war inside
Releasing this save me, you can't deal with this
I want to open up, I'm scared and worthless
I realize my only passage is to suffer and die

A pool of despair I've fallen into
No strength to save, myself a fool
See the fading glimpse of me, malevolent atrocity
Drowning in an unbeatable depression, to die or exist
Please answer this
Why does the warm water freeze as I try to swim ashore

Matthew De Latour

What Hate Can't Describe

Everlasting lies and hypocrisy remain
The only reflections of society
Confused sick pathetic beings of fluid
Failures only blaming each other, I hate you all
Sick humans who commit actions not worthy of animals
I truly reject all and will not conform and add to the problem
I'm not on this planet to procreate
Or have perverse entertainment
I'm here to save my soul, if I even have one

Society is dead; society has blood poisoning
Society has no sense of direction
Humans blame what ever they can, except themselves
We're not being punished, by a supernatural being
We're screwed for the same reason a hiker is lost in the woods
He lost his compass and can't see through the trees
We're lost because we have misplaced our compass
Misplace our morale

I don't know who I hate more, men or women
Men and women today are weaker, less reliable
Less willing to accept responsibility
Less able to endure discomfort or hardship
They won't postpone gratification and tolerate corruption
Women as a whole are less feminine than in the past
Men are less manly

I don't mean less sexually active, every guy can't wait
To go out and make a trophy out of some female
Just like a predator, men are less dignified
And are less self-reliant, they bitch more and whine more
Commitment and dedication are quite sparse

Shadow of Darkness

Women are trying to be men and forgetting their instincts
They have been raised with the attitude if men do it, then I can
There uniform now t-shirts and jeans, pathetic beings
They never cease to disappoint me

We need opposites, like positive and negative
Without these two there can be no flow of current
No balance and no normal behavior, what is normal
When we are all equal in all areas
There is no need for a mutual relationship, no need for skills
Only a sexual one is desired
This mutual silence is the cause for cheating
When sex is all you have, that's all you will have
That leads to boredom and finally suffering

I hate human stupidity
It's like leaving children responsible for maintaining a house
That's why this planet is shit
All divisions of the human race are now flawed
Their reproduction is no different that a disease spreading
To kill its next innocent victim
This wondering existence never stops with its attacks
What, who, when

The lazy, addicted, deceptive whores
My family and yours
Misguidance, the weakness of soldiers in battle
I'm sick, I'm too angry, I've shed blood and I wish I could again
Just to try and erase life's imperfections

I stand virtually alone in my quest
I find intelligent individuals along the way
Who also have come to realize the truth
So many more believe the lies, especially their own
If you don't believe what I have written

Matthew De Latour

And what you now are reading, then you're rejecting truth
Well the truth hurts
It will always be easier to swallow a comforting lie
Tolerance equals lies

I have one thing to overcome, waking up
I've been angry for years, my only defense
When you hate society, you reject hope of love
I haven't cried in nine years, sure I have had a few tears
At moments, but I honestly can't wail or cry like an infant
I wish I could, I've been so hard so long, I'm starting to fall apart
I have lost touch with so many emotions
Hatred will remain my love my passion
I have chosen a path, which I cannot leave
Maybe there is good ahead, maybe I might find my dark goddess
My gothic queen, to kneel before her
Catering to her needs
That's just a fantasy, that's how society thinks
I can't let my self wander into that trap
If I were to find someone good, a potential love
I would probably toss her aside and live with self regret
Until my demise

Shadow of Darkness

Nights Darkest Hour

In the night it comes to me, I control it for my own destiny
I've told it to kill, but now it kills when it is its time
I've called for some to die, but their still alive
Now it chooses who it wants to kill
It has stopped doing my will

In the darkest sky, in the blackest night
It comes and it wants to take life
Nothing will stop it; it only can kill
I fear for my life, it's stopped doing my will

Hell is now here; its growl sends a fear
Why did I lose control, now it does what it wants
It may cost me my soul
As the night grows darker, I try to hide
I hear it starting to kill; surely I will die

Flesh is tore away; it will only continue to bring death this way
Anger grows in this beast, as it continues its fight
Why did this have to happen tonight
I used to control it, but why didn't I quit
I guess I was a fool to even deal with it

Soon this creature of hell smells my fear
I come into its vision, shedding tears
Large blood stained teeth are the last thing I see
I never thought this could happen to me

She came that is no lie, because of me, many died
She only wanted to take life; nothing could stop her tonight
In the end it was me she wanted to kill
My girl friend stopped doing my will

Matthew De Latour

Within

Suffering, immoral hatred
Wickedness hooks, points calamitous
Blood pain sores
Perverse gruesome terrible lacerations
Scars, malice, spiteful deformed
Asocial, sick morbid, hate
Murder, disgust, thorns, cuts
Mute, dying, dead rotting soul

No Chances Given

Betrayed outer flesh paints its decree
While seeds are planted to grow in thee
Sprout forth the disaster within
Empty out the darkest of sins

Carry out the order given so long ago
Never decreasing in a steady flow
Burn with hatred until the meeting of death
Chant these words in final breath
Suicide is control

Matthew De Latour

Angel of Light

Sing, sing, Morning Star
Grant thee sacred knowledge from afar
Sing, sing, Morning Star
Grant thee sacred knowledge from afar

Bleed, bleed, Morning Star
Giveth thou unholy knowledge
Power from afar

Bleed, bleed, Morning Star
Giveth thou unholy knowledge
Power from afar

Bleed, bleed, Morning Star
Giveth thou unholy knowledge
Power from afar

Shine; shine Morning Star
Shine; shine Morning Star

Strike; strike Morning Star
Strike; strike Morning Star
Strike; strike Morning Star

Reficul, retne, refilcul, retne
So I may kill you
Shine; shine Morning Star
Soul taketh to the stars

By suicide the light hides what you are
The light hides who you are

Shadow of Darkness

Spread Drinking Piss

Tied to the body now
Bound so beautifully, how
Why such an urge to escape
Hands tied, spread open fate

Caressing, kissing full blue lips
Ball gag choking, broken hips
Opened hole exposed to see
Splendor passionate misery

Not yet dead, close to arrival
Existence in this vessel, no survival
This wide-open imperfection
Yet more pain hidden, not mentioned

Calm collective submission
No chance to make decisions
Glamorous spotlight decay
Never wanted to be here to stay

Left here for dead, no option
Here naked in a coffin
Sickness of this place, never to miss
To much time, forced drinking piss

Matthew De Latour

Another Death

Don't wait for life
Every second, everyday my words are pointless
Nothing to say, nothing that hasn't been said
Not trying to shock, you're dead

I'm dead; my tongue is dry
Voice is gone; spoke to long
Death still delights
Most of whom I adored lay dead
I could write a book about death
Time tears, seems like ancient years

Have you ever seen a woman give birth to a child
Then touching it, start to masturbate with the child
Thrusting its soft head into her bloody cunt
Firmly grasping the babies head with care, shoving it in
Mommy sensually moves her hips, feeding her hungry lips
Baby crying, mother cumming
Fucking herself, harder and harder like a passionate lover
Baby skin tearing, soft bones snapping
Vaginal lips craving, bleeding, swallowing

So wet, her clit is red and hard, pointing where to insert
Rigorously, faster, and faster, she moans with satisfaction
The baby flapping about
Blood flies in mommy's bright loving eyes
Gripping the infant sex toy in and out
Spatters, shoots orgasms in her babies mouth
I guess newly arrived humans do have a purpose
The bloody body of tiny lust now motionless, dead
Mom is satisfied, oh well another death

Holy Patricide

I hate you; I hate you
I hate everything about you
I hate anything of you
I hate your deception
I hate your rejection
I hate your face
I hate your dwelling place
I hate your anger
I hate you pretender
I hate your affliction
I hate your decisions
I hate your hostility
I hate your ambiguity
I hate your malevolence
I hate your lies
I hate your disguise
I hate your violence
I hate your dominance
I hate your stress
I hate your carelessness
I hate your hypocrisy
I hate you constantly
I hate your maliciousness
I hate your torment
I hate your fiendishness
I hate your grievousness
I hate your deprival
I hate your survival
I hate your sadism
I hate your voice
I hate your intolerance
I hate your repulsiveness
I hate your cruelty

Matthew De Latour

I hate your insanity
I hate your hysteria
I hate your demoralization
I hate your laceration
I hate your immoral mind
I hate you all the time
I hate your curses
I hate your killjoy
I hate your terror
I hate your impatience
I hate your verbalism
I hate your symbolism
I hate your brutality
I hate your mortality
I hate your presence
I hate your darkness
I hate your strife
I hate your life
I hate your pain
I hate your name
I hate your family
I hate your friends
I hate your possessions
I hate your ideas
I hate your stupidity
I hate your evils
I hate your birth into existence
I hate your soul
I hate you enemy
I hate everything out of your breath
I loved your death

Shadow of Darkness

Thursday The 12th

Lying here want to sleep, but the new hour is calling
Struggle to breathe, get up and face the horror of a new creation
Fearful, yet trying to relax, overwhelmed in chaos
What do I do

No desire to breath the air, angry already I don't care
Faces of misery continue to mock me, am I alone
What is reality, and does is matter what I do
Tell me are the voices true

Pain inside all over exploding into me, irritation can't control
Hating every object in view
Short of breath, my body aches to face another moment
I sit in darkness

How do I accept myself, I don't want to answer this
There is no peace of mind, can't escape and why try
Why can't I feel emotion, why can't I have something
I want to sleep forever

Irritated I continue my day, fear and hate of all and everything
I can't function with nervous thoughts, tormented by my own breath
I try to rest, but I can't close my eyes

Still lost in a series of thoughts, I can't take another one
Why do I think this way, sorrow and death are all I see
I can't take the lies and continuing discontent
My hatred of myself grows stronger and soon I hope it will end

Worthless in a no hope jar seeing everything from afar
My blood is all I want to see, covered in it only me
Try so hard just to care, all alone in my own despair

Matthew De Latour

When will this day end, I am not my friend

Soon darkness will come again and maybe I can see
Will I wake up and still hate me or will I suffer another day
Should I stick around to face my cries, the new day is now here
I'm too scared to open my eyes

Drop Out

I don't care what you can do to me
I'm no longer a member of society
I dictate my own laws
Do what thy will
I choose who I love
I choose who I kill

I won't follow any rules
Any lies thrown at me
I'm a drop out of society

They say conform to our human ways
I only see lust and confused desire
No love, not today
I won't respond to what a man is supposed to be
I may be sick, but not as sick as society

I won't follow any rules
Resist the lies given to me
I dropped out of society

Matthew De Latour

Born Out of Darkness

Image conception; disregard not to mention
The blackest of dreams, conceal the means
Counsel the mind, to mature with time
Events, the horrors of impressions made
Past is future, never to fade

Growth, hope to restrain
What actions caused bleeding brain
Spirit starved voice inside
No guarantee, only to die
Therapy, no answers, never forget
Each day reminded, past is met

Peace just a thought of the day
Anguish hurting, with nothing to say
Now vile, no hope granted
Grown sickness, from seeds planted
Questions from lies, years cry
Begging, screaming why
Left to die

Choices

Young are these days, as pain relieves the memories
That so haunted a weak spirit
Hardening and hiding emotion
The time of what, dead already

Cursed by words, bruised with dance
The bitter occasion of a mental relapse
Intellection, mind over matter
Hearts born with desire

Evil an option, subject to anything, controlled by everything
Safety is where
Stalk forever or become prey
Before crossing look both ways

Matthew De Latour

Backward Life

Mother, Father, bleed and cum
Thrust, scream, vociferation, compelled to torture
Masturbation, rotten foul, hopeful bowel
Corroborant cock, ass blood ejaculating some how

Finger filled little hole; dried rectum shit
Fetus head hanging out from it
Open mouth dripping with wet love
Forked tongue to see
Shoved in there, aborted, never free

Precious memories; touch and smell
A cock inside pumps cum against a beating heart
Backward, thoughts decent
Rape your parents

Some Unity

Society expanding from the start
Standing in the way of moral progressions
Is the lust of mans heart

Only willing to meet his own needs
Deserting friends and family
This can only work for a short time
Before we lose every thing
Soul and mind

Can't escape conformity
Your actions
The colors you where dictated by society
Why even try, in this time we live to die
Ejaculation Creations

Matthew De Latour

Forget This

Deceiving all, telling all
There's an answer, no there's not
Save my soul, save it for what
Tomorrow will never come

Never to have control
Never to be whole
Try and live
Live for what
Why, distant so close terror

Just one more lying lie
Just one more
Given, cursed, freely marked
What am I supposed to do

Hide, live, live in shame
Cry; die, in whose fucking name
Do I need to bleed just to get help
Will the bleeding stop
Like some fucking bleeding cunt
Hiding behind a pare of panties
Hide; lie, just to fucking die

Shadow of Darkness

The Endless Day

Unfulfilled dreams, visions turning to pours
Needles erect from them
Annihilated broken organism
Striving, not yet dead, blasphemous lips shut
By bleeding, desensitizing words

Magnified, obscured way of life
A decision already made and made useful
An embrace of violent, systematic aggression
That leads to a predicted end
While more pain sifts through a broken heart

Trying to understand this hypocritical double standard
A blemished misuse of organized beliefs
Buried to deep to find, to eventually reach a solution
Left over turning obstacles
While creating more problems

Disgusting, confused, careless minds; only wanting
Needing today, actions so powerful in this place
Wanting more and realizing the appropriate way
The way to conduct, to achieve ecstasy
Cease; forget all and every biological impulse that is desired

Surrounded in the sick swirl of society
Made to conform to lies of educated individuals
Controlling this shit hole
Open up, disregard all, hate, fill, and accept defeat of this battle
But continue to receive unknown knowledge
The force in the polluted air
Emotional gratification not seen, yet existing in all
Invisible actions of affection, find it
The color of your soul

Matthew De Latour

The Response

Neurosis open living mind war
Will not give in, anger consumes
Hours going by, dreams of more confusion
Terror unveiled, sickness approaching the core

Eternal hatred spilling out, spewing
Forth to erase visions of this world
Eyes bleeding onto a now painted corpse
Acting on impulse, seeing, doing

Filled glutton of pain, no remorse crying
Split down, organized to receive
Why this gift, now an object of hate
Breaking, hide, can't see me dying

Shadow of Darkness

Words Need Action

Hate, hate, hate, hate
Hate, kill, hate, hate
Kill, rape, hate, hate
What they've done
Words nothing, works something

Red everywhere
Hate, kill them, hate
Hate, hate, hate, hate
Man's greatest pleasure is injuring others
Hatred ever so pure, hate, hate, hate
Kill the red; rebuke the red

I wish I could crucify their religion
To the tree of knowledge of good
And evil and burn it
Into the soil from which it came

Who is the red
Sick mellow entanglement; crazy war cartoon
Controlled by meaningless words are today's youth
Overcome what words, words of what
Taken away all wisdom, freedom
Now a slow downfall
Die red die; kill a red

Decorate them with fearful smiles
Smell the lies; make us liars
With their truth, we can lie
Deceive a new generation
Salute the red, white, and who
Just kill the red

Matthew De Latour

Red scum everywhere red
Erase, stop, wipe away
Die red, our truth abducted
Left to starve, will we starve
We will on words alone

One Plus One

Confident almighty; inner dwelling being
What is inside of me
Chance to escape depart for a time
A shadow of me; quite opposite you see

With this blessed curse
I feel I have lost my mind
The feelings take over with time

Seeing through my eyes
They're not mine
Different actions, motions escape with their own will

Pleasant, glamorous personality always hidden
Now free, why even exist all this time
I must stop questioning my mind

Matthew De Latour

Violently Socialized

I woke up just the other day to see my face on
The front page of the newspaper, in my hand
Called life and so far I've been asked and told
What's your future hold, I read some more and
Looked for hope, but only saw failures, my sadness
In big letters, subtitles of life no longer fun
Can't you see just look at me, a dying body
Read some more and see, it said blood flows from
My wounds and sprays onto you, or any other reader
An expression my be required here, but I have none
Turn the page, possibly a bright future is ahead
I once saw it in your eyes, but now I'll see your demise
The paragraph replied, tragedy is what you're headed for
Put here to decay, have a nice day
The last page I turned to looked the same, me; myself
Rotting and starting to brake, I hope to find
Some dreams, but only nightmares remain
The final phrase of the ending line, me broken into
Pieces to fit into a sick puzzle of the world, life
Conform to this, the paper spoke, I then replied
Still wandering why

Me

Hate my choice, my desire
Putrefied madness expanding
Growing from within this obsessed
Neurotic mass of destruction
No sympathy exists, only revenge
Harvest my hate, dwell in the shadow

Hate my love; hate my addiction
Mercy a laughable word
Hate is the pleasure, the reason to live
Existing visions
Dominate my weak, strong, presentation of a man
Psychotic, sexual sociopath
Frustrated from this world, hated
Alone in my grave

Matthew De Latour

Erasing Life

Fighting, dreaming to gain control of the past
Our hour has come to rule at last
Sickened, thou hast ascended to where
Forever journey in humble prayer
Stirreth the unseen wisdom and put your trust in me
Rebuke; kill all the good in thee

Boast not thyself of tomorrow
For thou knowest not what day may bring sorrow
Forsaken in dark bliss
Alone grant me an unholy kiss
Of you, pain bound upon thy heart
Tied around the neck, never to depart

Abominations flow in the veins of howling
So harvest a prideful look, speak in a lying tongue
Shed only innocent blood
Wickedness own thy soul
Run to mischief, soweth sin before my throne
Burn with hatred so the light consumes
Never dimming, brighter than crescent moons

Curse into the darkness
Where weeping and gnashing of teeth descend
Dream of pleasure, worship within
O thou adversary, cast unto me
Consider my trouble, which I suffer for thee
Drink of many things black, serving yourself
Trespass against all, rebuking there every call

Consumed where midnight shall fall
Desecrate the bowel of those who brought you in this place
Where no vessel ever escapes alive, death remains

Shadow of Darkness

Resist temptations of the pure; rape their trust like a whore
Opening wide, your presence be known
Appear without fear, as we march into battle
To slay these beings who move as cattle
Words of vengeance be our cry
To live forever, while our enemies die

Matthew De Latour

Everyday Reality

I find myself staring at any random object
For what seems like an eternity
Perfectly still like an on the guard statue
Absorbed with pain and fear and I cannot cry
It seems I have forgot how

Shadow of Darkness

An Extra Note

How did this happen, my life taken away from me
I lost my innocence; I can never be free
You took all my hope and love
Striped it all away, told me every idea I ever had
Should be throne away

I am bleeding inside; I have no place to hide
No friends ever to turn to
Took my innocence I can't forgive you

Everyday it's all the same, curse me out
Take all the blame; tell me I'm a fool
I'm worthless, study for school
A mistake you being born
I told you stop, you've been warned

I am bleeding inside; I have no place to hide
No love ever to turn to
Took my innocence I can't forgive you

Why hate everything I do, I used to try to please you
You spit in my face, bitched me out and called me a disgrace
Never could I do it right
I can't remember one happy night
Because of you I have no self-esteem, no love
It's only a dream; I wish all this on you
How could you be so cruel

I am bleeding inside; I have no place to hide
No hope ever to turn to
Took it all, I can't forgive you

Now all my thoughts are anger, all this because of you

Matthew De Latour

Now I hate everyone, especially you
I lost my soft heart, you made me evil and dark
I wish I would die, maybe then you would cry
This pain you caused, I hope you see
It is still inside of me

Shadow of Darkness

They're Just Words

Any words, more worlds
Looking back, trip into a forgotten time
Careful what you will find
Blood hole or shit hole, past intent evil
Overriding the frail shaped, bleeding mind
So many sorrowful wounds, abundantly
Distributed in careful order, sex sells death
No longer hidden, because you're dead
No more could fit into the head
Raped a cop, should have called back up
They're just words
Confident intriguer, live and die
Metaphorically speaking
In a modern society children are killed
Sodomize the mother with pieces of her child's flesh
They're just words
She must now shit her child out
Well, shit it out
Shit it fucking out honey
Shit the kids remains out of that tight little asshole
You thought you killed your child
You really killed yourself
They're just words

Matthew De Latour

Kreation

In this place I'm a deteriorating vessel
Blandished by evil, made dismal
Giving all of myself, to face this place
Trapped and irritated, I remain mortificated

When you see me in this place, broken
What is in me, I'm ashamed
Want to be free, erase all of me
Forget what I am, woeful man

I don't wake up to see the sun rise in this place
I wake up because I can't fall back to sleep
To dream, to forget this secondary, sick
Omnivorous place of hostile confusion; that I hate

Existing in a place, where I can't reveal my face
Determined to leave forever, nothing to remember
Sick of all of it, I don't want it
Disembodied I quit

Finished Project

Young rewired brain, permanent affects
Dramatic shifts in personality
Self-destructive actions, hormones changed

Impaired capacity
To develop appropriate emotional responses
Neurons connected wrong
Growing emotional problems

Small corpus callosum
Limbic system disturbed
Now sick and in shame

Nowhere to belong
Depleted chemicals, mute screaming personality
Can't continue with life
No more trauma

Matthew De Latour

Senseless Existence

Conceived into this present state
To a moment, an existence in which you hate
A presence within your vessel not permitted to mention
Where is the escape to release the tension

Many have like you
Gone to accept this unknown, like a common cold
Living ashamed until you grow old
Cutting yourself open, just to see what's inside
Maybe there's an answer, to know why you're alive

Hiding what can't be seen, anger an emotion
Is it really what you mean
Hating, reject yourself; refuse to see
Blood drips from your confused body

Your primary hidden pain
Locked into a dying frequency
Corresponding with unknown changes
Where counterpoint self-destruction
Leaves you again questioning this inner conflict

Mind within; no free will to choose
Brought to a senseless life you can't refuse
Creation or mistake, what are you
You're no longer ashamed to lie about the truth

Yet this sickness within you goes on
A force of guilt much to strong
Still no answers for what you've accepted
Was there ever pleasure in this life demented

Existing in a pointless world

Shadow of Darkness

Where you take your first breath and you're already sick
Persecuted for what you tried, but could not fix
Convicted for problems you wish to die
A senseless existence, Why

Matthew De Latour

Last Plea

All around near and within, penetrating again and again
Numerous hidden ideals of what makes us exist
Forever unaware, feasting on dead fruit
Quenching our thirst with piss

Wandering in lies, this deception of life
Reservations in blackness forever night
A judgment will come upon us all
Light will rise, dark shall fall

Ancient wickedness that thrived for so long
Teaching us the secrets, dance and song
Elements we still cannot grasp, instilled within
How much longer can we last
Punishment for unholy lives
Vaporous evil ideas, what we made life

This perverted constituted legal system of hypocrisy
Each year we change our moral
Justify what once was obscene
Hidden and brought forth, rebuked and now glorified
Glory and truth laughed at like lies

A spiritual conspiracy claiming every soul willingly
We have no remorse for our actions
We now reward sinful self-gratification
I cry out to be pure and true, but I stand unclean the same as you

Help, oh glorious God above, King of Kings
Righteous perfect being, for you I sing
Shed your wisdom and patience upon me
Light my way, set me free
Make the impossible, possible on this day

Shadow of Darkness

Take my pain; throw it away
Oh God above, I want to see
Will you ever smile on me

Matthew De Latour

The Final Cessation of Vital Functions

Looking around, burdened each and everyday
Subject to receive a constant pain
Entrapped in this dissolute time
Wounds are opened, destroying the mind

Assaulted by verbal razors, an attack not seen
Another scar, a new reason to hate society
Why constantly abusive every single day
It's always done in such a vivacious way

The violence used like sandpaper
Masticating a soft skinned red bleeding body
Tissue peeling, soon rotting
Taking with it all hope and emotion
This subcutaneous process done in regulation

Left now only to bleed to death
Tried so hard with every step
Incapable of overcoming the fear
Alone fighting for all these years

Never wanted, should have died in the womb
Slowly decaying, will be leaving soon
With no love, peace, or joy the vital attire
Worthless remains, now expired

Message from the Author

Salutations!

I arrived here March 6, 1982. These are my writings from age 16-21.

I didn't plan on publishing them. I recently just decided on the idea.

Maybe there are some individuals who may enjoy these poems. Well let my words be your voice. If you loved my book, thank you.

If you despised it, remember these poems are really just the words of a pissed off teenager. Well enjoy the rest of today.

La Mort Viendra!

Bon Au Revoir!

Printed in the United States
21190LVS00001B/166-204